Messages Without Words

Words by Barbara Sundene Wood
Professor of Communication
University of Illinois at Chicago Circle

Raintree Childrens Books
Milwaukee ● Toronto ● Melbourne ● London

Library of Congress Number: 77-27848

5 6 7 8 9 0 85 84 83

Printed and bound in the United States of America.

Library of Congress Cataloging in Publication Data

Wood, Barbara Sundene.
  Messages without words.

  (Read about)
  Bibliography: p.
  Includes index.
  SUMMARY: An introduction to various symbols, sig-
nals, and ways of sending messages that may be used to
communicate information. Includes such things as
alphabet, bells, facial expressions, flags, and smoke signals.
    1. Communication — Juvenile literature. [1. Communication]
I. Title.
P91.2.M6   001.5   77-27848
ISBN 0-8393-0084-0 lib. bdg.

Messages Without Words

When you send a message to someone, you usually say it or write it. Before people could write, they drew pictures on the walls of their caves. They often drew pictures of the animals they hunted. The pictures were the symbols of those animals.

totem pole

beauty symbol

A symbol is like a picture of a thing or an idea. People have used symbols since ancient times. Native Americans carved poles and then painted symbols on them. These pieces of wood are called totem poles. A totem pole tells the history and legends of the family it belongs to.

Some African women have a symbol for beauty. They believe it will help their children be beautiful.

hieroglyphics

The ancient Egyptians wrote with picture symbols called hieroglyphics. Each picture stood for a different sound. They put the hieroglyphics together to make messages.

Our alphabet today started out as pictures like these. The letter *A* probably began long ago as a picture of an ox. As time passed, different nations used that picture in their alphabets. It changed over the years to the *A* we use today.

Egyptian

Phoenician

Greek

modern

Many religions use symbols. The Star of David is a symbol of Judaism. The cross is a symbol of Christianity.

cross

Companies use symbols called trademarks. Trademarks help people remember the company. The symbols are usually simple. This is so people will remember them easily.

**Woolmark
pure wool**

Shell

Michelin

Few people could read in the Middle
Ages. So the people who owned shops used
symbols that everyone could understand.
Each kind of shop had a special symbol as
its sign. Can you guess what people do for a
living in the shops in this picture?

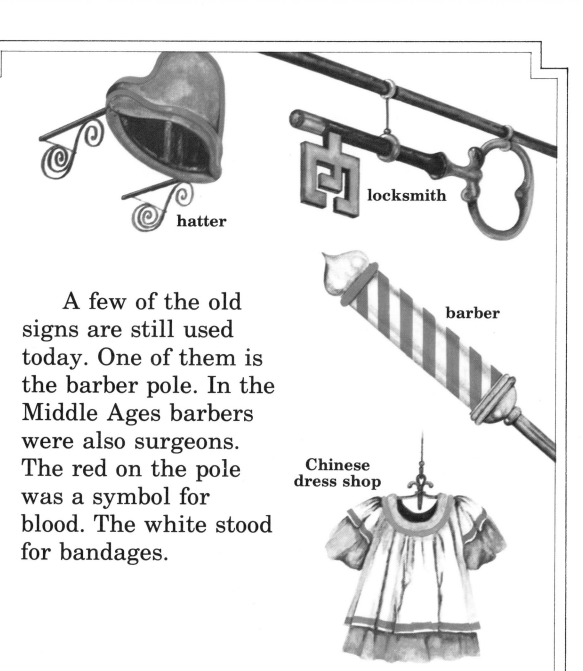

hatter

locksmith

barber

Chinese dress shop

A few of the old signs are still used today. One of them is the barber pole. In the Middle Ages barbers were also surgeons. The red on the pole was a symbol for blood. The white stood for bandages.

In the Middle Ages, knights wore armor. It hid their faces and bodies and protected them. The only way you could recognize knights was by looking at the patterns on their shields. The pattern was called arms. The same pattern was sewed on their coats and on the cloth coat of their horses. The coat was called a coat of arms.

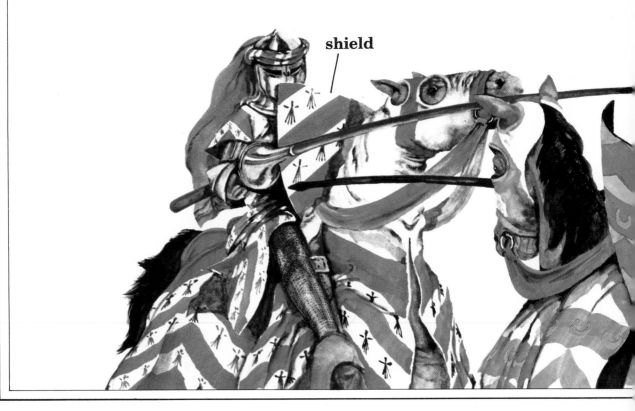

shield

Each family had its own coat of arms. It was a symbol of the family. Through the years it ws handed down from each father to his children.

the old arms of France

the lions of England

coat

Countries can also have a coat of arms. Richard the Lionhearted wore these three lions on his coat of arms hundreds of years ago. They have been part of the British Royal Arms ever since. What do the lions mean to you? Maybe it meant they were a brave family.

Olympic flag

Flags are symbols. Every country has
its own flag. The flag of the Olympic Games
has at least one color from every flag in the
world. A flag is treated with respect
because it is the symbol of a whole country.

The green on Brazil's flag is a symbol of its forests. The yellow diamond shape stands for its minerals.

The sickle on the flag of the Soviet Union is a symbol of its farmers. The hammer stands for its factory workers.

There was a dragon on the flag of the Chinese empire. It was a symbol of wisdom and friendliness.

The flag of Cyprus shows the shape of the island. The olive branches are a symbol of peace.

Some flags send messages about the countries they belong to.

Ships use flags to send messages to each other. Each flag has a special meaning. Several flags can be put up at one time to send a message with many parts.

There are many ways to send messages without using words. Roman soldiers waved torches at night to give orders to attack from far away. Their enemies might have used fires to call for help when they knew trouble was coming.

Native Americans used smoke signals to send messages. They could read the messages from far away.

The light from a
lighthouse can send
a signal to ships. It
warns them to stay
away from dangerous
rocks. If ships are in
danger at night, they
shoot bright flares
into the sky.

Animals can be used to carry messages. At one time Paris was surrounded by enemies. It was hard for the French soldiers to get messages back and forth to their friends outside. So they put boxes of pigeons into balloons. The balloons flew out of Paris. The soldiers outside tied messages to the pigeons' legs. The pigeons flew safely back into the city with messages.

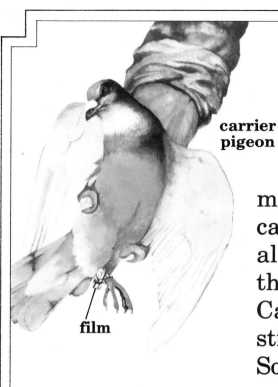

**carrier
pigeon**

film

Pigeons that carry messages are called carrier pigeons. They almost always find their way home. Carrier pigeons are still used today. Sometimes they carry messages on small pieces of film.

Messages can be sent using sound. This Amazon Indian beats on a buried tree trunk. A few miles away, another Indian puts his ear against another buried trunk. He can hear the signals and understands the message.

Some Africans send messages by beating on drums. The messages travel quickly from village to village. In a few days a message can be sent thousands of miles.

In Europe church bells ring out messages. The bells can be warning signals for the people. Or the bells can give information to them by the number of rings.

When we talk to someone, we use our voice to send messages. The other person must be able to hear our sounds. Deaf people can't hear these messages. So they learn to "hear" with their eyes instead. They talk to each other with hand signs.

Hand signs stand for words and ideas. Here are some signs and the words they mean.

sad   I   love

sign language

When deaf people
use sign language,
they can send
messages as fast as
people who talk and
hear. Sometimes
they know what your
mouth is saying
even though they
can't hear you. They
call this reading
your lips.

International Morse code

A ●━	M ━━	Y ━●━━
B ━●●●	N ━●	Z ━━●●
C ━●━●	O ━━━	1 ●━━━━
D ━●●	P ●━━●	2 ●●━━━
E ●	Q ━━●━	3 ●●●━━
F ●●━●	R ●━●	4 ●●●●━
G ━━●	S ●●●	5 ●●●●●
H ●●●●	T ━	6 ━●●●●
I ●●	U ●●━	7 ━━●●●
J ●━━━	V ●●●━	8 ━━━●●
K ━●━	W ●━━	9 ━━━━●
L ●━●●	X ━●●━	0 ━━━━━

Morse code is a way to send messages by sound or light. In Morse code, each letter of the alphabet has its own signal. The letter signals are made of short and long sounds. A short sound is called a dot. A long sound is called a dash. SOS is a well-known cry for help used by ships and people in danger. The Morse code for SOS is 3 dots, then 3 dashes, then 3 dots. Sometimes flashes of light are used instead of sounds.

People don't need words to send messages about how they feel. The expressions on their faces can tell you. The expressions for happiness, sadness, anger, and surprise are the same all over the world.

Actors can tell stories using just their faces and bodies. This is called mime.

Dancers use mime too. Their movements show if they are angry, happy, or sad.

Actors and clowns sometimes wear
costumes or paint their faces. Their faces
and clothes are signals to the people
who are watching them. These signals tell
the people who they are and what they
are feeling.

The Maori warriors of New Zealand were fierce. They marked their faces with tattoos. They made frightening faces and would stick out their tongues to scare their enemies.

Maori warrior

When we move our bodies so that others understand what we mean, we are using gestures. Gestures are ways of saying ideas without words. Do you know what these gestures mean?

Indian woman

Clothes can tell us things about people. Clothes can tell us where a person comes from. Sometimes clothes show what kind of work a person does.

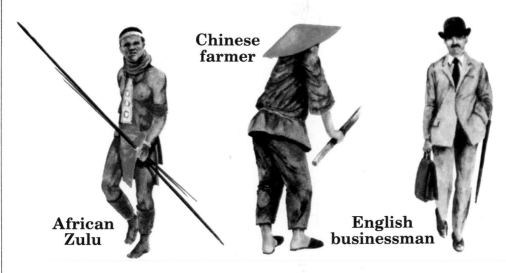

African Zulu

Chinese farmer

English businessman

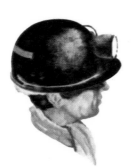

miner   **racing car
driver**   **police officer**

The helmets of the miner and racing car driver tell us their jobs are dangerous. You can tell who police officers, fire fighters, and soldiers are by their uniforms. The symbols on a soldier's uniform show what rank he or she holds.

**British Infantry
lieutenant**

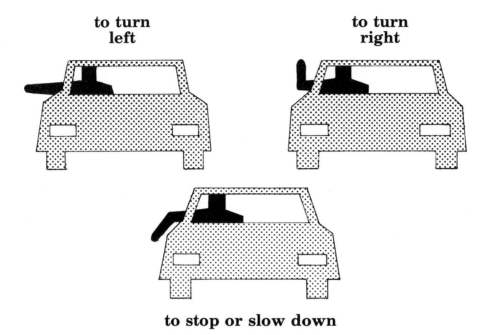

to turn left

to turn right

to stop or slow down

Signs, lights, and gestures send messages as we travel. Drivers can use hand signals to show other drivers what they are going to do. The lights in the back of a car show that it is slowing down or turning. Traffic lights tell drivers to stop, slow down, or go.

hill

school crossing

deer crossing

slippery when wet

Road signs show drivers which way to go. The signs warn of danger that might be ahead on the road. The sounds of car horns or sirens are signals that mean "Watch out!" These signs and signals are simple so that they are easy to understand.

The Metric System

In the United States, things are measured in inches, pounds, quarts, and so on. Most countries of the world use centimeters, kilograms, and liters for these things. The United States uses the American system to measure things. Most other countries use the metric system. By 1985, the United States will be using the metric system, too.

In some books, you will see two systems of measurement. For example, you might see a sentence like this: "That bicycle wheel is 27 inches (69 centimeters) across." When all countries have changed to the metric system, inches will not be used any more. But until then, you may sometimes have to change measurements from one system to the other. The chart on the next page will help you.

All you have to do is multiply the unit of measurement in Column 1 by the number in Column 2. That gives you the unit in Column 3.

Suppose you want to change 5 inches to centimeters. First, find inches in Column 1. Next, multiply 5 times 2.54. You get 12.7. So, 5 inches is 12.7 centimeters.

Column 1	Column 2	Column 3
THIS UNIT OF MEASUREMENT	**TIMES THIS NUMBER**	**GIVES THIS UNIT OF MEASUREMENT**
inches	2.54	centimeters
feet	30.	centimeters
feet	.3	meters
yards	.9	meters
miles	1.6	kilometers
ounces	28.	grams
pounds	.45	kilograms
fluid ounces	.03	liters
pints	.47	liters
quarts	.95	liters
gallons	3.8	liters
centimeters	.4	inches
meters	1.1	yards
kilometers	.6	miles
grams	.035	ounces
kilograms	2.2	pounds
liters	33.8	fluid ounces
liters	2.1	pints
liters	1.06	quarts
liters	.26	gallons

Where to Read About
Messages Without Words

Pronunciation Key

a	a as in **cat, bad**
ā	a as in **able,** ai as in **train,** ay as in **play**
ä	a as in **father, car,** o as in **cot**
e	e as in **bend, yet**
ē	e as in **me,** ee as in **feel,** ea as in **beat,** ie as in **piece,** y as in **heavy**
i	i as in **in, pig,** e as in **pocket**
ī	i as in **ice, time,** ie as in **tie,** y as in **my**
o	o as in **top,** a as in **watch**
ō	o as in **old,** oa as in **goat,** ow as in **slow,** oe as in **toe**
ô	o as in **cloth,** au as in **caught,** aw as in **paw,** a as in **all**
oo	oo as in **good,** u as in **put**
o͞o	oo as in **tool,** ue as in **blue**
oi	oi as in **oil,** oy as in **toy**
ou	ou as in **out,** ow as in **plow**
u	u as in **up, gun,** o as in **other**
ur	ur as in **fur,** er as in **person,** ir as in **bird,** or as in **work**
yo͞o	u as in **use,** ew as in **few**
ə	a as in **again,** e as in **broken,** i as in **pencil,** o as in **attention,** u as in **surprise**
ch	ch as in **such**
ng	ng as in **sing**
sh	sh as in **shell, wish**
th	th as in **three, bath**
t̲h̲	th as in **that, together**

GLOSSARY

These words are defined the way they are used in this book

actor (ak′ tər) someone who acts out a part
  in front of a group of people
alphabet (al′ fə bet′) the symbols that make
  up a written language
ancient (ān′ shənt) from long ago; very old
anger (ang′ gər) a strong feeling against
  a person or thing
armor (är′ mər) a hard covering that
  protects the body
bandage (ban′ dij) a long, thin piece of
  cloth that is tied around a hurt place
  on the body
barber (bär′ bər) a person who cuts hair
beauty (byoo′ tē) a quality that makes a
  person or thing pleasing to look at
blood (blud) the red liquid that runs
  through the body
body (bod′ ē) all of a person; everything
  you can touch

British Royal Arms (brit′ ish roi′ əl ärmz) the arms which belong to the king or queen of England

bury (ber′ ē) to cover up; to put under the ground

carve (kärv) to make something by cutting wood with a knife

cave (kāv) a large hole in the ground or in the side of a hill

Chinese (chī nēz′) having to do with China

Christianity (kris′ chē an′ ə tē) the religion that follows the teachings of Jesus Christ

costume (kos′ tōōm) special clothes worn in order to look like someone or something else

cross (krôs) a structure made of one upright bar and another bar across it; a symbol of Christianity

dancer (dan′ sər) someone who dances; a person whose work is dancing

deaf (def) not able to hear

diamond (dī′ mənd) a very hard mineral

draw (drô) to make a picture in outlines

drum (drum) a hollow instrument that makes a sound when it is beaten

empire (em′ pīr) a group of countries under one ruler

expression (eks presh′ ən) the outward appearance; the look on a person's face

factory (fak′ tər ē) a building or group of buildings where things are made

film (film) a special material used to take photographs

fire fighter (fīr′ fī′ tər) a person who puts out fires

flare (fler) something that burns with a sudden light

gesture (jes′ chər) a movement of the body that shows what a person is thinking or feeling

hammer (ham′ ər) a tool with a heavy head, used for hitting nails

helmet (hel′ mit) a hard hat or covering which protects the head

hieroglyphic (hī ər ə glif′ ik) a symbol that stands for a word or sound; the kind of symbol used in ancient Egyptian writing

history (his′ tər ē) the story of events that have happened in the past

information (in′ fər mā′ shən) the facts about something

island (ī′ lənd) a piece of land that is surrounded by water

Judaism (jōō′ dē iz′ əm) the religion followed by the Jews

knight (nīt) a fighting man in the Middle Ages

language (lang′ gwij) the spoken words used by a group of people

legend (lej′ ənd) a story that is handed down through the years about a person or thing

lighthouse (līt′ hous) a tower with a strong light, built near the sea to warn ships of danger

Maori (mau′ rē) the native people of New Zealand

meaning (mē′ ning) what a thing means

Middle Ages (mid′ əl aj′ iz) the time in the history of Europe from about A.D. 400 to 1450

mime (mīm) a performance where people use gestures without words to act out a situation

miner (mīn′ ər) someone who works under the ground in a mine

mineral (min′ ər əl) a substance that can be found in the ground or water and can be used for many things

movement (moov′ mənt) an act of moving

nation (nā′ shən) a land or group of people under one government

national (nash′ ən əl) belonging to a nation

olive (ol′ iv) belonging to a tree which has small, round fruit

Olympic (ō lim′ pik) having to do with a group of athletic events in which many countries take part

ox (oks) the male of a kind of cattle

pattern (pat′ ərn) a certain order of objects, shapes, or colors

peace (pēs) a time when there is no fighting or war; quiet, calm

pigeon (pij′ ən) a bird with a small head and rounded body that is found in the wild and in most cities

rank (rangk) a person's place or standing in an ordered group

recognize (rek′ əg nīz′) to know what something is when you see it

religion (ri lij′ ən) a system of ideas and beliefs about God and life

respect (ri spekt′) to think well of a person or thing; a polite way of acting

Roman (rō′ mən) belonging to the empire of ancient Rome

sadness (sad′ nəs) the feeling of being sad

shield (shēld) a piece of armor carried by knights in the Middle Ages to protect them

sickle (sik′ əl) a tool with a curved blade, used for cutting down plants

simple (sim′ pəl) easy to understand

siren (sī′ rən) a loud whistling noise used by police cars and others to give warning that they are coming

soldier (sōl′ jər) someone who fights in an army

surgeon (sur′ jən) a special kind of doctor who does operations

surround (sə round′) to be all around; on all sides of

tattoo (ta tōō′) a colored pattern on skin

tongue (tung) the part in the mouth which moves when we eat or speak

torch (tôrch) fire or flame used as a light

totem pole (tō′ təm pōl) a wooden pole that has symbols carved or painted on it

trademark (trād′ märk′) a symbol used by a company to identify the things it makes

travel (trav′ əl) to move from one place to another; to go on a trip

treat (trēt) to act in a certain way toward something

understand (un dər stand′) to know the meaning of something

uniform (y$\overline{oo}$′ nə fôrm′) special clothes worn by members of a particular group

wall (wôl) a flat, upright side of a structure

warning (wôrn′ ing) a message of trouble or caution

warrior (wôr′ ē ər) someone whose work is fighting

wisdom (wiz′ dəm) knowledge and understanding

write (rīt) to make letters and words with special symbols on some surface

Bibliography

Bolian, Polly. *Symbols: The Language of Communication.*
New York: Franklin Watts, 1975.

Castle, Sue. *Face Talk, Hand Talk, Body Talk.*
Garden City, N.Y.: Doubleday and Co., 1977.

Charlip, Remy, and Beth, Mary. *Handtalk: An ABC of
Finger Spelling and Sign Language.* New York:
Parents Magazine Press, 1974.

Chester, Michael. *Deeper Than Speech: Frontiers
of Language and Communication.* New York:
Macmillan Publishing Co., 1975.

Dugan, William. *How Our Alphabet Grew.* Racine,
Wis.: Western Publishing Co., 1972.

Goaman, Muriel. *News and Messages.* North Pomfret,
Vt.: David and Charles, Inc., 1973.

Lubell, Winifred, and Lubell, Cecil. *Picture Signs
and Symbols.* New York: Parents Magazine Press,
1972.

Rinkoff, Barbara. *Red Light Says Stop!* New York:
Lothrop, Lee and Shepard Co., 1974.

Thomson, David. *Language.* Morristown, N.J.:
Silver Burdett Co., 1975.